Russian Translator: Dmitriy Vvedenskiy

This is a parody book.
There is no actual content.

About the author:

Tony Darnell is the author of *Twenty Forty-Four: The League of Patriots*, a disturbing view into the future of society where a single political group has almost complete control over every aspect of the daily lives of the citizens. This political group is known as the Party, and the citizens they control welcome the promise of security over freedom. The people are completely unaware of the liberties they have relinquished under the guise of equality for all.

A covert group, known as The League of Patriots, seeks to overthrow the government and return the country to a place where the citizens enjoyed and revered the freedoms and liberties of the past. The mission isn't an easy one, as the Party will certainly imprison or kill any of the participants if they are discovered.

David Gagnon faces a dilemma. After deciding to join the League of Patriots, he is offered a promotion at work which includes a higher salary and a beautiful assistant. Struggling to achieve his mission objectives, he is torn between fulfilling his duties and cultivating a relationship with Stephanie. Will he be able to complete his part of the mission before being captured or killed by the Party, and will the League of Patriots be able to restore freedom and liberty to his country?

The series explains how society could evolve to a state where every action is monitored and recorded, where there are no written laws, and even negative thoughts against the Party are a crime. *Twenty Forty-Four* looks into the future and explains how society could succumb to total government control over every aspect of life, unless The League of Patriots succeeds in their mission.

For more information, see: http://2044thebook.com

THE ELECTION CRIMES OF
DONALD J. TRUMP

EVIDENCE OF HIS
COLLUSION WITH RUSSIA

Chapter 1

The following is the evidence of Donald J. Trump's collusion with the Russian government in order to influence the 2016 Presidential election.

(This section intentionally left blank)

This page intentionally left blank.

This page intentionally left blank.

This page intentionally left blank.

This page intentionally left blank.

This page intentionally left blank.

This page intentionally left blank.

This page intentionally left blank.

This page intentionally left blank.

This page intentionally left blank.

This page intentionally left blank.

This page intentionally left blank.

This page intentionally left blank.

This page intentionally left blank.

This page intentionally left blank.

This page intentionally left blank.

This page intentionally left blank.

This page intentionally left blank.

This page intentionally left blank.

This page intentionally left blank.

This page intentionally left blank.

This page intentionally left blank.

This page intentionally left blank.

This page intentionally left blank.

This page intentionally left blank.

This page intentionally left blank.

This page intentionally left blank.

This page intentionally left blank.

This page intentionally left blank.

This page intentionally left blank.

This page intentionally left blank.

This page intentionally left blank.

This page intentionally left blank.

This page intentionally left blank.

This page intentionally left blank.

This page intentionally left blank.

This page intentionally left blank.

This page intentionally left blank.

This page intentionally left blank.

This page intentionally left blank.

This page intentionally left blank.

This page intentionally left blank.

This page intentionally left blank.

This page intentionally left blank.

This page intentionally left blank.

This page intentionally left blank.

This page intentionally left blank.

This page intentionally left blank.

This page intentionally left blank.

This page intentionally left blank.

This page intentionally left blank.

This page intentionally left blank.

This page intentionally left blank.

This page intentionally left blank.

This page intentionally left blank.

This page intentionally left blank.

This page intentionally left blank.

This page intentionally left blank.

This page intentionally left blank.

This page intentionally left blank.

This page intentionally left blank.

This page intentionally left blank.

This page intentionally left blank.

This page intentionally left blank.

This page intentionally left blank.

This page intentionally left blank.

This page intentionally left blank.

This page intentionally left blank.

This page intentionally left blank.

This page intentionally left blank.

This page intentionally left blank.

This page intentionally left blank.

This page intentionally left blank.

This page intentionally left blank.

This page intentionally left blank.

This page intentionally left blank.

This page intentionally left blank.

This page intentionally left blank.

This page intentionally left blank.

This page intentionally left blank.

This page intentionally left blank.

This page intentionally left blank.

This page intentionally left blank.

This page intentionally left blank.

This page intentionally left blank.

This page intentionally left blank.

This page intentionally left blank.

This page intentionally left blank.

This page intentionally left blank.

This page intentionally left blank.

This page intentionally left blank.

This page intentionally left blank.

This page intentionally left blank.

This page intentionally left blank.

This page intentionally left blank.

This page intentionally left blank.

This page intentionally left blank.

This page intentionally left blank.

This page intentionally left blank.

This page intentionally left blank.

This page intentionally left blank.

This page intentionally left blank.

This page intentionally left blank.

This page intentionally left blank.

This page intentionally left blank.

This page intentionally left blank.

This page intentionally left blank.

This page intentionally left blank.

This page intentionally left blank.

This page intentionally left blank.

This page intentionally left blank.

This page intentionally left blank.

This page intentionally left blank.

This page intentionally left blank.

This page intentionally left blank.

This page intentionally left blank.

This page intentionally left blank.

This page intentionally left blank.

This page intentionally left blank.

This page intentionally left blank.

This page intentionally left blank.

This page intentionally left blank.

This page intentionally left blank.

This page intentionally left blank.

This page intentionally left blank.

This page intentionally left blank.

This page intentionally left blank.

This page intentionally left blank.

This page intentionally left blank.

This page intentionally left blank.

This page intentionally left blank.

This page intentionally left blank.

This page intentionally left blank.

This page intentionally left blank.

This page intentionally left blank.

This page intentionally left blank.

This page intentionally left blank.

This page intentionally left blank.

This page intentionally left blank.

This page intentionally left blank.

This page intentionally left blank.

This page intentionally left blank.

This page intentionally left blank.

This page intentionally left blank.

This page intentionally left blank.

This page intentionally left blank.

This page intentionally left blank.

This page intentionally left blank.

This page intentionally left blank.

This page intentionally left blank.

This page intentionally left blank.

This page intentionally left blank.

This page intentionally left blank.

This page intentionally left blank.

This page intentionally left blank.

This page intentionally left blank.

This page intentionally left blank.

This page intentionally left blank.

This page intentionally left blank.

This page intentionally left blank.

This page intentionally left blank.

This page intentionally left blank.

This page intentionally left blank.

This page intentionally left blank.

This page intentionally left blank.

This page intentionally left blank.

This page intentionally left blank.

This page intentionally left blank.

This page intentionally left blank.

This page intentionally left blank.

This page intentionally left blank.

This page intentionally left blank.

www.ingramcontent.com/pod-product-compliance
Lightning Source LLC
Chambersburg PA
CBHW030249030426
42336CB00009B/307